plant
forage
make

PUBLISHED BY
REBECCA DESNOS

Plant Forage Make is independently published by Rebecca Desnos.

rebeccadesnos.com / info@rebeccadesnos.com

Instagram: @rebeccadesnos

ISBN 978-1-7398197-2-9 (paperback)
ISBN 978-1-7398197-3-6 (eBook)

Published by Rebecca Desnos, in 2022, in the UK.

Photo on the front cover is by Rebecca Desnos.
Photo on the back cover is by Bex Partridge.

"Flowers are the music of the ground.
From earth's lips spoken without sound."

– Edwin Curran

Hi! I'm Rebecca Desnos, a natural dyer in the UK, a writer, mother, and an all-round plant lover.

I'm an independent publisher who is passionate about sharing a love of plants with others!

Get in touch

Do you have any comments or questions about Plant Forage Make? I'd love to hear from you!

info@rebeccadesnos.com

Portrait by Siobhan Calder / Background photo by Aaron Burden

Welcome!

I'm thrilled to be back with the second volume of Plant Forage Make. This edition is themed around *Colour*. As a plant dyer, of course this was a way to squeeze in as many natural dye projects as possible - and if you turn to page 44 you'll even find a tutorial for making watercolour paints from earth! But more than that, it's been an opportunity to delve into the botanical world with fresh eyes and learn lots of new things from the amazing contributors.

Every magazine I create is a personal passion project that I slowly work on over a few months and I truly savour every moment. As I sat at the laptop during the cold, winter evenings (with my baby Rose asleep in the carrier) an image that kept popping into my mind was friends sitting in a garden, trying out different projects - like a fun, crafty meet up! I hope you're able to share the joy of plants with others this year.

Now it's spring, this new publication is about to be born into the world. That's when the exciting part begins and I have the joy of sharing the ideas on these pages with you!

As always, thanks so much for supporting my projects. I feel so lucky to be an independent publisher!

Rebecca x

Vol. 1 Plant Forage Make, and all of my other publications are available in print and as a digital downloads via **rebeccadesnos.com**

97

68

91

82

87

heavenly hydrangea

78

33

56

36

contents

44

27

60

Introducing the contributors

Victoria Stevens grows plants for food and joy. She has a specific interest in social and therapeutic horticulture and botanical crafts. She writes about gardening for wellbeing and creativity. Find Victoria's article about developing your own therapeutic garden on page 15.
growcreatejoy.co.uk

Latifat Apatira is a California-based botanical nature printmaker. Guided by her faith and a life-long curiosity about plants, Latifat uses fresh flowers and foliage, ink and watercolour to create unique flora portraits. Her work weaves art, botany, and history, and encourages others to tangibly explore the depths of their own personal connection to the botanical world. Read Latifat's interview on page 19.
titilayola.com

Liz Spencer is an artist, maker, natural dyer, gardener, educator and mother. She was a venture fellow at the Brooklyn Fashion & Design Accelerator and holds an MA from the London College of Fashion. She taught at Parsons the New School and The Fashion Institute of Technology and has continually shared natural dyes in public workshops since 2012. Liz guides us through setting up a dye garden on page 27. **thedogwooddyer.com**

Katie Whittington is a writer, mother and maker. She lives in the Lake District, UK, with her family. She loves wild swimming, foraging, natural dyeing and hiking. Katie shares a personal story about the colour blue on page 33.
instagram.com/katie.whittington

Clara Infante is a multidisciplinary maker and artist based near Barcelona, Spain. She explores plant and earth pigments often manifested through sculptural wax creations. On page 44, Clara guides us through the process of making watercolour paints from earth pigments. **shopcopito.com**

Colleen Codekas is passionate about healthy living through natural food and herbal medicine. She likes to go foraging for wild edibles and mushrooms, cook delicious food, make mead, grow an incredible amount of edible and medicinal plants, and make herbal medicine. She is the author of the book *Healing Herbal Infusions*, four ebooks and runs online foraging courses. Read Colleen's interview on page 56. **growforagecookferment.com**

Tara Lanich-LaBrie is a herbalist, chef, forager, artist, and gardener, pairing her love of plants with her love of creating and sharing food. She started *The Medicine Circle* nearly a decade ago to celebrate creating beauty, medicinal food, sharing seasonal recipes, and building community around the love of plants. Tara teaches courses on culinary herbalism and foraging, and writes monthly articles and eBooks. Learn about butterfly pea flowers on page 60 and find Tara's rainbow pancake recipe on page 65. **themedicinecircle.com**

Suzie Grieve is a wild weaver based in the Lake District, UK, who creates wild baskets and jewellery from foraged fibres. Suzie works on a miniature scale and gathers vines, bark and stems throughout the year to weave into tiny vessels. Read an interview with Suzie on page 68. **foragedfibres.co.uk**

Harmonie O'Loughlin is the mama maker behind Flora's Feast. You can find her in the garden growing herbs, in the kitchen experimenting with plants, or her nose in a herbal book. Follow for herbal tidbits, recipes and more at **@florasfeastbotanicals** or discover her shop and blog at **florasfeast.com**. Harmonie shares a couple of springtime recipes on pages 75 and 78.

Lorene Edwards Forkner is an author, maker, and speaker whose work centres on exploring the wonders of the natural world. Lorene writes a weekly gardening column for *The Seattle Times*. Her latest book, *Color In and Out of the Garden, watercolor practices for painters, gardeners, and nature lovers*, has just been published. Lorene shares how to begin a new daily art practice by observing nature and recording colour swatches. **ahandmadegarden.com**

Alice Griffin is an author and poet with a gypsy soul. Right now she is wandering the waterways of England aboard her narrowboat, Melody. She leads seasonal e-courses to bring us back to nature, and ourselves. Alice shares a touching story with us on page 87. **alicegriffin.co.uk**

Bex Partridge, founder of Botanical Tales is the author of *Everlastings: how to grow, dry and create with dried flowers* and *Flowers Forever*, and can be found on Instagram **@botanical_ tales** as well as on **patreon.com/botanicaltales** where she offers insights and learnings about growing, drying and creating with everlastings. Bex shares some amazing tips with us on page 91. **botanicaltales.com**

Susan Beech is a paper artist specialising in the making of crepe paper flowers. She founded her studio *A Petal Unfolds* in 2016 and her book has just been released: *A Petal Unfolds - How to Make Paper Flowers*. Make your own cosmos flowers by following Susan's tutorial on page 97. **apetalunfolds.com**

Becky Searle is an ecologist, botanist and kitchen gardener best known for combining science with gardening. She encourages others to grow food using natural processes to become more organic and sustainable. Becky believes that understanding a little of the science behind ecosystems and plant growth can make gardening easier and more enjoyable! Read about colourful plants and pollinators on page 102. **sowmuchmore.co.uk**

PLANT FORAGE MAKE

Safety notes

- Take care when identifying plants and mushrooms and if you need guidance, consult a reliable book or a knowledgeable friend.
- Natural does not always mean safe, so always be moderate in your use of plants and herbs as food and medicine. Please only taste plants you can identify with 100% certainty, and do not touch toxic plants. If there is any doubt at all, do not touch it.
- Please consult a herbalist for treating with herbs.
- The recipes in this book are for enjoyment purposes only – not to treat any health conditions.
- Get permission from the landowner before gathering anything.
- Make sure you harvest plants that are clean and free from chemicals, animal and human urine or faeces. This is why permission is important, as the landowner may be able to inform you if any chemical pesticides have been used.
- When you try homemade skin care products on your body, do a patch test first.
- When you are heating dye pots, make sure you have good air circulation. Keep a window open and don't stand over a steaming pot and breathe in the vapour. Wear gloves to protect your skin. Use a separate set of equipment for dyeing, i.e. not your kitchen pots.
- When working with earth pigments, stick to ochres in the form of loose earth, as grinding unidentified rocks can be potentially dangerous as some are toxic. Stones and earth may have levels of toxicity which may be harmful to your lungs after repeated exposure so please wear a mask while processing these and work in a well ventilated area.

PLANT FORAGE MAKE

"Reading about nature is
fine, but if a person walks
in the woods and listens
carefully, he can learn more
than what is in books..."

-- George Washington Carver

PLANT FORAGE MAKE

Getting 'away' in the garden

Create your own soothing and uplifting garden, no matter how much (or little) growing space you have. Whether a spacious outdoor area, patio, balcony, window boxes or even an indoor windowsill, we can all benefit from pulling nature to us.

Words and photos by Victoria Stevens

One of the many gifts of a garden is that it offers a sense of being 'away'. Even in the most urban areas, we can escape the hardness of the city, the artificial environment of the workplace and the stresses of everyday by surrounding ourselves with greenery. Increasingly, gardens are being created in hospital grounds and around office blocks to give the people who use them the mental restoration that comes from being close to nature.

Using plants, you can make a soothing and uplifting space, no matter how much room you have to grow. You don't need a sizable garden, in fact you don't need a garden in the traditional sense at all to have your very own 'away' place.

Whether a spacious outdoor area, a patio, balcony or windowsill, we can benefit from pulling nature to us. In a medium to large garden, 'rooms' can be created for different purposes such as a relaxing, sitting area or a section that's bright and cheery. With containers in a courtyard or balcony, you can curate your own ever-changing scenery all year round. This is creative freedom not afforded to planting in a bed. Have fun arranging the display in tune with the plants' current form and to please your eye. With window boxes or pots on a windowsill, you can create a pleasing view of greenery against the sky above, forming a natural buffer between you and the world beyond.

Keeping a garden of any kind can bring

varying degrees of activity or rest. Both experiential or interactive elements of gardening stimulate our senses, which help divert our attention away from feelings of anxiety, stress and low mood. Whether our bodies are working hard or at a gentle pace, our minds fall into the quiet rhythm of the life around us.

Consider your own lifestyle, health and physical needs when planning your garden. If you don't have lots of time or energy to look after a large area or plants that require continual attention, then you will need to make a smaller, low maintenance 'away space'. In any case, a great joy of gardening is the element of play it brings into our lives. As adults we are rarely afforded the time to take part in activities just for the love of doing them. Hobbies are often pushed aside as our expanding 'to do' list of work and domestic obligations take priority. But we can play by spending time nurturing and enjoying plants. Because of the ever-changing habit of nature, we can allow ourselves to fall into it, let go of control, enjoy the process, experiment and be surprised.

" Viewing green scenery can lower our heart rate and cortisol levels (both indicators of stress)..."

When it comes to choosing plants for colour, the foliage itself can often be overlooked because of course green is the most abundant. However, studies of nature's effect on stress have clearly shown that viewing green scenery can lower our heart rate and cortisol levels (both indicators of stress) and help recovery from illness more quickly than viewing other types of scenes. This is great news for anyone growing houseplants, which exhibit an assortment of feathery, lush, spiky, dense, trailing and glossy leaves in all shades of green.

Indoor windowsills can become a theatre for jolly violas, salads, herbs and microgreens, which are all edible too. Outdoors, grasses of different heights and small evergreen shrubs are low maintenance, yet they will gift you beautiful details providing interest through the seasons. Some grasses change colour and in autumn, slipping from green to yellow, while others flower with cream, fluffy tipped stems that catch the sunlight and almost sparkle. Other varieties will make a rustling sound in the breeze.

These are the moments to capture when creating a garden: an amazing canvas that affords ever-changing art to see, smell, touch, taste, feel and experience. Aesthetic preferences are very subjective and similarly, what invokes positive feelings of safety, happiness and calm will also vary from one person to another. You may be drawn to a busier wildflower style or kitchen garden, or you might favour a modern or minimalist design. There's no doubt that the options are wide and varied but there are a few things to bear in mind when choosing plants and colour schemes for your space.

"Right plant, right place" originally coined by garden designer Beth Chatto is one mantra that gardeners will repeat over and again. This simply means that we should grow plants where the conditions are right for them to thrive. After that you have a world of options to choose from.

Foliage is not only green but ranges from silver through to deep red; when the flowers bloom, this is when colour truly comes alive and dances. Flowers are usually more transient than foliage, so bear this in mind when selecting plants for the whole season. Similarly, it is worth considering the life span of plants in your garden and whether they are evergreen, deciduous or herbaceous. This will affect not only the seasonal structure and display but also the way you maintain and develop your space.

Growing annuals means you get to sow seeds and nurture young plants into the soil every year, arguably the most enriching role you can take as a gardener. With so much variation, it is tempting to grow plants and flowers of all colours of the rainbow. This is entirely your choice and it's your time to explore and find what you love. However, following a few colour principles will help you achieve a particular feel or atmosphere for your space.

Planting complementary colours side-by-side creates an uplifting tone and harmonious combinations are more soothing. The wider the range of colours, the more energetic the design, whereas fewer colours offer a calmer feel. A monochromatic scheme may seem a little flat but with a contrasting accent colour the dynamic is instantly changed. Hot and deep colours invoke a sense of being drawn closer, yet cool, pale colours open up a space. As the light reduces during the day and through the seasons, some colours recede and some glow. In the brighter light of the summer, some colours wash out and others positively shine like stained glass windows.

The most important thing to remember is that there are no right or wrong choices. Nothing is permanent and plants can be moved, replaced or repeated season upon season. With a garden of any kind, we are never working towards one final result, instead we are taking a journey where we will always learn and be rewarded and no time will ever be wasted. 🌿

The art of nature printing

Foraged plants, ink and watercolour.
Discover how Latifat Apatira creates
stunningly realistic botanical prints.

Words and photos by Latifat Apatira

You do a very unusual form of printmaking called botanical nature printing. Can you tell us more about this, including the history of the technique?

Nature Printing is an ancient printmaking technique that uses natural objects to produce images on cloth or paper. Before photography, botanical nature-printing was a tool used by physicians, botanists, and naturalists to document exotic and medicinal plants. It was less expensive than hiring an illustrator and produced remarkably detailed images.

It is theorized that nature printing began in the Late Middle Ages. Leonardo da Vinci (1452–1519), in his *Codice Atlantico* included a nature print of a sage leaf. In the 1700s, Benjamin Franklin designed currency sheets with botanical nature prints as a counterfeit deterrent around the time of the American Revolution. And in Japan, the art form of Gyotaku (gyo "fish" + taku "impression") dates to the mid-1800s and was used by fishermen to record their catches.

While many techniques have been developed through the ages to create prints, ranging from candle flame soot to electroplating, my process is very simple. I apply black ink to fresh flowers and foliage and then I hand press the plant's inked image onto watercolour paper. The resulting image is then hand coloured, creating beautiful and life-sized botanical artwork that utilises the natural form and textures of the plant.

What attracted you to nature printing in the first place?

Nature printing merges art, botany, and history and I find all three topics fascinating. The first time I recall reading the term "nature printing" was in a newsletter published by a local garden that offered botanically based craft courses. I was flipping through the pages, enjoying the photographs of spring flowers and I saw an announcement for a *"unique mixed-media workshop."* The listing promised that students would leave the workshop with *"a gorgeous work of art reminiscent of antique botanical prints."*

Something inside me clicked and I knew I had to take that workshop. Despite it being expensive and held on a weekday (I have a regular job), I knew I was meant to be in that class. It's hard to describe my immediate fascination. So, I made it happen. For two days I experimented with plants, ink and watercolour and created art that I was proud of! While I had always been a plant enthusiast, I was shocked at how much I hadn't previously appreciated in terms of detail and texture. That workshop focused and forever changed the course of my creative journey and enriched my awe of the botanical world. I have been creating prints, learning and refining my process quite obsessively ever since.

When you add the watercolour layer to your prints it brings them to life in such a spectacular way. What's your favourite part of the process and why?

I love all aspects of nature printing. It starts with being in nature, surrounded by green, in the sunshine or fog. Being outside is always uplifting to my spirit. The scientist in me relishes learning about roles plants play in our ecosystem. I research their common and scientific names, folklore and ethnobotanical uses, and most importantly, if they are edible!

Hand colouring is a special part of the process, but it's also the scariest. I can very easily ruin a beautifully composed ink print with colouring that I'm not satisfied with. But when it turns out well, the portrait animates and permanent life is returned to the ephemeral. The art now has a story to tell.

PLANT FORAGE MAKE

Can you share a little bit about your connection with nature? Does your love of plants go back to your childhood?

I grew up in California's beautiful Bay Area and every weekend my parents would take my brother and I on hikes through the vast open spaces of the peninsula. We explored oak woodlands, coastal scrublands, redwood forests and the oceanside. I was always collecting objects found in nature – rocks, feathers, shells, pinecones. I pressed flowers and photographed them with my simple 35mm camera. At university, I studied Integrative Biology, and took a course on medical Ethnobotany, the study of plants used in traditional medicines around the world. It was the best class I took during my eventual nine years of university and

graduate education. Plants and nature have always played central roles in my life.

How do you feel while you're creating your art?

Printing today remains as fulfilling as it was at that first workshop. I love the meditative state of being in "creative flow". I can stand all day at my printing table until my back hurts and I'm physically exhausted, and still come away feeling alive and wonderfully accomplished.

I am a Muslim and, in my tradition, God informs me through the Holy Qur'an to pay attention to the signs of wonder all around us. When the inked plant is lifted, I am always astonished by the beautiful

intricacies of pattern and venation revealed to the point I now see the extraordinary in every "ordinary" leaf and flower; all wondrous signs of The Creator. And with that realisation, I am mindful and grateful.

Do you have any favourite places to gather plants?

I don't have a favourite place to gather. I've collected the most wonderful passion flowers from the side of a busy highway! I do think it's important to gather plants with respect to ensure that plenty is left for other people, animals, birds, and bees to enjoy. I only harvest plants that I can identify which avoids taking rare or protected species. I typically gather a few leaves and flowers, and rarely forage whole plants unless it's growing in obvious abundance. Lastly, I ask for permission before harvesting on private property or on public lands. I'm always surprised at the incredible generosity and support of others.

How can someone else learn how to make nature prints?

I teach a few in-person and online classes a year. You can check out my website for upcoming workshops, at **titilayola.com.**

Also, an internet search of *"how to make a nature print"* will provide excellent family-friendly resources. For those interested in more detailed instructions on the array of nature printing techniques, the Nature Printing Society's Guidebook, *The Art of Printing from Nature*, is a comprehensive manual – **natureprintingsociety.org.**

Is there anything else you'd like to share about you or your work?

What I enjoy most about nature printing is that it is an accessible art form. One that is unassuming, approachable, and no previous art experience is necessary to achieve rewarding results. Unlike botanical illustration or wood block printing, creativity through this art form can be explored without the need to draw. I hope that my art will inspire others to cultivate an intentional awareness of the diversity of plants around them. With imagination, curiosity and creativity, nature printing can be an amazing method for us to explore the depths of our personal connections to the botanical world. 🌿

PLANT FORAGE MAKE

"I think that no matter how old or infirm I may become, I will always plant a large garden in the spring. Who can resist the feelings of hope and joy that one gets from participating in nature's rebirth?"

– Edward Giobbi

PLANT FORAGE MAKE

Planning a dye garden

Whether you're an established or new natural dyer, I heartily recommend starting a dye garden to reap the colour joy of getting to know natural dye plants more intimately. Many dye flowers offer beautiful colour and textural variety to the established ornamental garden.

Words and photos by Liz Spencer

When choosing which plants to grow, first, find out your "why"...

I have grown dozens of different types of plants exclusively for dye over the past ten years and suggest that if you're feeling overwhelmed by all the possibilities for growing colour, you first establish *why* you want to grow your own dye, and which colours are of value to your artistic practice. Here are some questions to help guide you:

Are you hoping to extract dye for creating dye baths?

In this case you will want to prioritise 'yield' of colour from plants in your dye garden and grow plants with the potential to make more dye per square foot of growing space. For instance, in most climates, Japanese Indigo *(Persicaria tinctoria)* will produce more indigo pigment than woad *(Isatis tinctoria)*, but for hotter, more humid climates, Indigofera (e.g. *Indigofera suffruticosa)* plants may be the ideal plant to grow for maximum blue dye yield.

Are you more interested in direct application for plant shape and colour play through techniques like bundle dyeing and eco-printing?

Many plants like coreopsis *(Coreopsis tinctoria)*, purple pincushion flower *(Scabiosa Atropurpurea)* and black eyed susan *(Rudbeckia hirta)* offer fantastic dye from all parts of the plant stem to leaves to flowers. Plus they also dry nicely after harvesting for storage and future off-season dyeing.

Is light fastness of colour very important to you?

If so, then I strongly suggest making that a priority when researching your dye plants. If there's a historic textile heritage tradition that has employed a plant for dye, it's highly likely the colour this plant will create can endure through the years on your future heirlooms.

Get to know your immediate climate character to better understand what types of plants will thrive for you: simply knowing your plant hardiness zone and expected annual rainfall will help you determine when to start seeds and what to expect for the growing season.

Look at your local colour history

Many plants used for dye are of multifaceted ethnobotanical use: connect with your local native plant nursery and research literature to find out about historic use for local plants in your area. You may already have dye plants in your garden or yard that live there for other edible or medicinal use – hello pomegranate tree or rhubarb leaves! And importantly, please respectfully honour and support local indigenous groups. Seek wisdom, if you can, by taking workshops and paying for the knowledge that has been honed and held for generations.

A starter dye garden

Almost any plant can be used by the dyer but it is a few specific plants that give vibrant and lasting colours in the colour families of blue and red that I suggest seeking out. True light fast purples and greens can then be achieved by over-dyeing and layering colour with the many yellow-producing dye plants; yellow is certainly nature's favourite dye colour!

For instance, in a mild or temperate climate, I suggest weld for yellow, Japanese Indigo for blue, and madder root for red. Then additionally a few varieties of dye flowers such as sulphur cosmos, coreopsis and purple pincushion flower can really fill out additional opportunities for creative play with techniques like eco-printing and bundle dyeing.

If space is limited, some plants can be grown in window boxes, balcony planters, or stoop side and in big pots. One advantage to container growing is the ability to move your plants if need be to accommodate their light needs. I've successfully grown Japanese indigo, *Indigofera suffruticosa*, cosmos, coreopsis, madder, and marigold in pots. Potted plants need more frequent attention, but the colour reward can be great!

Weld *(Reseda luteola)* is the most light fast yellow dye whose colour comes from the whole plant, especially the flower heads. This plant can be easily dried and saved for winter dye projects. I have a long growing season so I may be able to see flower stalks emerge in the first year, but weld is typically a biennial, flowering in the second spring after sowing seed.

Madder (*Rubia tinctorum*) sits among others in the Rubia family such as *Rubia peregrina* and *Rubia cordifolia* as a reliable red-producing plant for dye. I've grown madder from cuttings and seed, so even if you can't find seeds (they can be tricky to germinate if older than 1 year) you could ask around in your community, social media dye groups or textile guilds to see if anyone else is growing madder from which you may take a root and stem cutting. Two-year-old roots give red dye as well as shades of pink, salmon, orange and terracotta.

Indigo – Indigofera (*Indigofera suffruticosa*), Japanese Indigo (*Persicaria tinctoria*) and woad (*Isatis tinctoria*). This year I'm growing 3 different species of indigo bearing plants.

Persicaria tinctoria is the easiest to grow in my mild coastal climate in Southern California. I water often as the plants mature, but once in the ground they do well with a weekly deep watering. If you grow in an area with long hot humid summers you might consider trying to grow a variety of Indigofera.

Woad will be growing in my garden for the first time in a few years. Although the potential indigo content for this plant is much less than with Japanese Indigo or Indigofera, the plant itself offers unique leaf shapes with which to use for leaf print making and the seed shape and colour are particularly beautiful for bundle dyeing. This plant is noxious and invasive in many western states in the US, so be very mindful about harvesting seed in the spring. Woad is a biennial which means the seed comes the following spring after the first growing season.

Weld-dyed fabric

Homegrown madder root

Fresh indigo dye on wool and silk

A coreopsis flower

Silk dyed with cosmos

pH sensitive dye
made from purple
pincushion flowers

PLANT FORAGE MAKE

Bonus dye garden plants

Cosmos - After 6 years of growing sulfur cosmos (*Cosmos sulphureus*) exclusively for dye, this year I'm trying 8 different unique cosmos species including homegrown 'sulfur', and other deep coloured flower varieties such as 'Rubenza' and 'Candyfloss' (*Cosmos bipinnatus*) and the rare 'Black Magic' (*Cosmos atrosanguineus,* also known as 'Chocolate Cosmos'). Cosmos is incredibly easy to grow, can be cut and harvested for months on end, attracts pollinators galore and can be very hardy and drought tolerant once established. They make fantastic flowers for paint-making, immersion dye baths, solar dyeing, bundle dyeing and eco-printing. They're a powerhouse in the natural dye garden that I include every year.

Coreopsis (*Coreopsis tinctoria*), an indispensable part of my dye garden. This native American wild flower is easy to grow and giving beyond belief of hundreds and hundreds of potent dye flowers. As with some other dye flower plants, the whole plant top including stems and leaves can be used for dye, making it an excellent choice for those looking to eco-print plant shapes. I pick the flowers all summer long to dry and save for future dye projects and then harvest the whole plant top at the end of the growing season to either dry for future dye or extract straight away for colours of golden brown, orange and yellow. This year I'm growing a mix of red and yellow flowered coreopsis as well as a few other varieties with interesting colour and pattern possibilities including 'Desert Coral' and 'L'il Bang'.

Purple Pincushion Flower (*Scabiosa atropurpurea)* was a new-to-me plant for the dyepot in 2015 when I first started growing it in my garden. I had never seen it referenced in any publication on natural dyeing, but after seeing the incredible teal colour on a stack of textiles in the studio of fellow dyer Kristin Morrison of All Species Studio, I decided I had to grow it! Like black hollyhock, and Hopi black sunflower seeds, the dyes created by this specific variety of pincushion flower are classified as 'anthocyanins' making them less light fast, but still fun to employ.

It's a great dye to use with children because of its pH sensitivity: a colour, art and science lesson just waiting to happen. Use bicarbonate of soda (baking soda) and lemon juice to transform one dye extraction into many different colours. It's a fantastic flower for eco-printing because the beautifully shaped leaves are also full of yellow flavonoid dyes. They dry easily to save for future dyeing, and each flower head is made up of dozens of individual florets that can be sprinkled for speckled effects in bundle dyeing. I have also very much enjoyed using purple pincushion flowers for making anthotypes (sun bleaching prints), which I teach in my online workshops. 🌿

Further exploration

Liz's course *A Year in Natural Dyes* is an in-depth natural dye education with a new focus each month. **thedogwooddyer.com**

PLANT FORAGE MAKE

Photo by Pure Brittney Strange

Blue eyes

Reflections on indigo,
motherhood and the colour
blue in nature.

Words by Katie Whittington

Eye colour is determined by the amount of melanin in the iris. Blue eyes are not blue, they are in fact an absence of brown. Blue pigment in nature is similarly an illusion: rare, precious, a trick of the light. The striking blues you see on birds and butterflies are not made from pigment; they are structural colouration. Peacock feathers are brown but their structure makes them reflect iridescent blues and greens. The sky is not blue. Blue is a trick. The one exception to this in the animal world is the obrina olivewing butterfly: the only known animal that can produce a true blue pigment.

The first time I saw some blue Himalayan poppies I fell in love with their translucent sky-blue petals. It is the purest blue I have seen in a flower. Blue flowers produce their colour through tricks with light and blending the pigments responsible for reds (anthocyanins). The blue poppy tweaks its anthocyanins to appear blue by altering its pH levels and using metal ions. The rarity of blue flowers is a consequence of the great lengths they go to, to achieve their colour.

Recently, I heard about the discovery that all blue-eyed people have one common ancestor who lived more than 6,000 years ago. Everyone with blue eyes is technically related. As an adoptive parent, this is something I enjoy knowing. Our family all have blue eyes, mine and my daughters are a particularly piercing forget-me-not blue. It's something people still pick up on when searching for a likeness. Strangers will say, *"You've got your mummy's eyes"* in passing, and I will smile.

A few summers ago, when my eldest daughter was just a toddler, I decided to try indigo dyeing. Preparing a vat of indigo and dyeing the fabric is a long process, taking almost two days, but once I saw that magical transformation for the first time it was worth all the effort, and I was hooked. I loved the way the dye took differently every time depending on the varying conditions of the vat and the different fabrics I used. To my delight, after following instructions meticulously, my first vat was successful. I was entranced as I plunged my fabric into the pot of bubbling blue, breaking the oil-slicked surface, I watched as it instantly turned into an acid yellow-green colour. Even more magic came when I pulled it out carefully and hung it up on the line to oxidise, the green gradually turned to a pale, then darker, blue with the wind's breath, like the flames of summer licking at spring. My daughter would often come out into the garden to watch this last phase, delighting in the magic and learning for herself there and then that there is no blue without green.

Centuries ago, before indigo, the only available pigments for dyeing and painting were earthy shades of brown, yellow and red. The rarity of blue pigment made it all the more revered when it was discovered, often being called blue gold. Not only is indigo one of the most vibrant natural dyes, but it is also one of the most colourfast and is completely unique as it needs no mordant or heat to bond to the fabric, instead this is achieved through a carefully balanced chemical process involving pH levels and oxidisation.

Why are so many of us drawn to the colour blue? Perhaps because of its ability to make us feel it is of another world, just beyond our reach. Blue is hard-fought in nature: a clear bright sky, a blue moon, the first bluebell of spring, a blue dawn. How magic that the rich depths of indigo are made from a few simple green leaves? How clever the forget-me-not is, to lure us in with its trickery. How beautiful my daughter's eyes are, reflecting light and love. 🌿

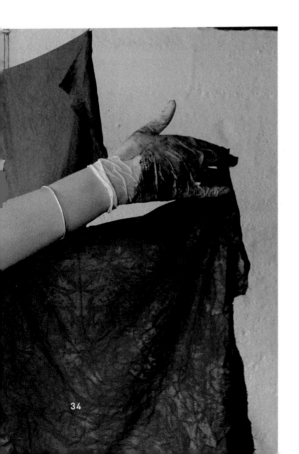

" *Everyone with blue eyes is technically related. As an adoptive parent, this is something I enjoy knowing.* "

PLANT FORAGE MAKE

Photos by Katie Whittington

Grow your own indigo

Words and photos by Rebecca Desnos

Grow and dye with indigo on a tiny scale. Try it, and you just might fall in love with this plant...

Small scale

This is an invitation to grow your own Japanese indigo plant (or small group of plants) and dye yourself something special. Try it first on a tiny scale to get a taster for this incredible dye plant, and next year you might choose to grow more plants from your saved seeds. You can dye a tiny scarf with just a handful of leaves or scale up.

We will be using the "salt rub" method which involves rubbing salt into fresh leaves, and rubbing the juicy mixture into fabric. This technique originates in Japan and is an easy way for growers to use indigo on a small scale. I learnt about this method in a You Tube video by the film maker Ryoya Takashima, where he visited the Ohara Koubou dye studio in Kyoto, Japan.

Persicaria tinctoria

Japanese Indigo and Dyer's Knotweed are the common names for *Persicaria tinctoria,* which is a frost-tender member of the knotweed family. This semi-tropical plant likes a lot of sun. In the UK it can be grown from seed to flower in the spring through to autumn, and it dies when the temperatures drop later in the year. The leaves contain indigo.

Growing your plants

If you're short on space, you can grow Japanese indigo on a small scale. Start your plants indoors, and once the risk of frost has passed, grow your plants on an outdoor windowsill or balcony. Your indigo babies may even grow on a very sunny indoor sill, but is quite tricky to 'over winter' indoors, and better to just sow more seeds the following spring.

These instructions are based on my climate in the UK, so you'll need to adapt this for different locations.

I start my seeds at the beginning of April, and drop 5-6 seeds into little plant pots filled with multipurpose compost. You can use a tray with little modules, but I often use paper plant pots or toilet rolls cut in half and filled with compost. I learnt this 'multi sowing' method (several seeds per little pot) from no-dig gardener Charles Dowding. He uses this method for growing vegetables and herbs, and it works great for Japanese indigo too!

The seeds need warmth and light to germinate, so I put the tray of paper pots in a clear plastic bag to make a mini 'greenhouse', with some holes for air flow. Then put the tray on a warm windowsill or use a heat mat. This creates a warm, moist microclimate. I find a heat mat helps the seeds germinate quicker. On a windowsill, it has taken 3-4 weeks for the seeds to sprout, but on a heat mat I have seen signs of life within a week or so. Fresh seeds give the best germination rates.

Once the seeds have started to sprout, remove the plastic bag and ensure the seedlings get as much light as possible. Keep indoors as frost will kill these tender plants. Once the plants have grow an inch or two, 'pot on' into a larger pot with more multipurpose compost. Keep nurturing them with regular watering and plenty of sunlight.

In the UK, I wait until the end of May or even the beginning of June before I plant them in the garden. My last frost date is mid-May. Search online to find your average last frost date and use this as a guide.,

Choose a sunny position for your plants – ideally somewhere that gets sun most of the day, but I've still had success on a north-west facing balcony that only had sunshine from the late afternoon onwards. No matter what kind of growing space you have, it's still worth trying.

When you plant your indigo babies outside, make a hole with a 'dibber' or a small trowel, and bury the plants so the stems are below the soil level and just the leaves are exposed. Water the plants well. They should now grow happily in their new home.

Water regularly – the exact frequency will depend on your climate and weather. You can poke your finger into the soil and if it's dry below the surface level then water. They are quite a demanding plant, so I find they do much better when watered regularly. As warmth-loving plants, they grow even better in a greenhouse or polytunnel. If you grow "under cover" then you can plant them out earlier as they will be more protected from frost.

After a couple of months, when you start to see some good growth, you can take your first little harvest. When you cut the stems, this stimulates the plant to grow more, just like when you cut herbs.

As a guideline, It's best to dye with the leaves before they flower, as after this point they are known to contain less indigo.

PLANT FORAGE MAKE

Your first dye experiment

When you're ready to dye with your Japanese indigo leaves for the first time, choose a tiny scarf, handkerchief, swatch of fabric or other small garment (such as a baby hat!). It must be made from natural fibres, although a small percentage of elastane is fine. If it's wool or silk (animal protein fibres) then you can just wash and dye it.

If it's made from a plant fibre such as cotton, linen or hemp, it's best to pretreat in soya milk. The protein acts as a binding agent between the fibre and dye, helping us achieve darker colours and improving colour fastness. You don't need to do this to silk or wool because they are already protein fibres.

Prewash your fabric

Simply wash the fabric at 40°C in the washing machine with natural laundry liquid.

Pretreat fabric in soya milk

This takes a bit of time and some forward-planning, but is worth the effort. The basic method for soya milk pretreatment is to dilute the milk in water at a ratio of 1:5 milk:water. In a mixing bowl or small bucket, soak the fabric for 12 hours, spin out the excess liquid in the washing machine, then hang to dry. When dry, briefly dip the fabric into the diluted milk, dry, then dip and dry again. Then ideally leave the dry fabric to cure for a week before dyeing. This allows the soya protein to bond to the fibres.

PLANT FORAGE MAKE

Dyeing your fabric

Cut a few stems from your plants. I've done this with just 5g of leaves and dyed a beautiful baby hat. Whatever you pick will be worth it for a pretty blue hue.

Pick the leaves off the stems and drop them into a bowl. Ideally use a bowl that's not used for food, as this is best practice for any natural dyeing, and the bowl may get stained if there are any scratches in the glaze.

Weigh your leaves. It doesn't matter how few you have, but it's interesting to know the amount for comparison purposes for next time.

Now comes the fun part. Either wear some rubber gloves (thin ones give you the best dexterity) or just accept that you'll have blue hands for a few days!

Add salt to your bowl of fresh leaves. When I have less than 50g of leaves, I usually start with 1 teaspoon of salt. You will need more salt for more leaves. Then start scrunching the leaves in your hands and the leaves will begin to shrink immediately. In a short while you should begin to notice some frothy green juice dripping out of your hands. If the leaves feel very dry, then add another teaspoon of salt to the mixture and keep scrunching and rubbing. Keep doing this until you have a wet, dripping ball of green leaves.

Then add your dry fabric to the bowl. The juice will immediately stain the fabric green. Begin to massage the leaves into the fabric and the colour will start to turn more of a teal. Keep rubbing and massaging, and continually moving the

fabric in your hands to try to get an even shade all over.

Carry on massaging and scrunching the leaves into the fabric until there is no more juice.

Depending on how many leaves you used in relation to the amount of fabric, your result may be mottled. In this case, you could pick some more leaves and even out the colour, or just accept your naturally marbled pattern. If you start with damp fabric, this may also give a more even colour.

Notice how the colour deepens after a short while – this is the indigo oxidising. It will become even more blue after washing later.

Rinsing out the chlorophyll

Let the fabric dry for the rest of the day or until the morning, then rinse in a bowl of water. The water will be bright green as the chlorophyll washes away. The indigo will oxidise more, and you should be left with a pretty shade of pale blue/teal.

Other tips

When you have very few leaves, scrunch the leaves and dab on fabric to make a pattern. Much like sponge painting that you might have done as a child, you can make mottled prints on fabric with a ball of squished indigo leaves.

Try painting with the juice from the scrunched leaves. When you add salt to

PLANT FORAGE MAKE

your bowl of leaves and begin squeezing, notice how the mixture becomes very juicy. Instead of adding fabric at this point, pour off some of the juice and use it as paint! It works well on paper and fabric (remember to pretreat fabric with soya milk).

Regrow the stems

You can make more plants from the stems you cut by putting them in water. When they have started to root, plant them outside alongside your other indigo plants, and you'll soon have more leaves to harvest.

Saving seeds

Depending on your climate, the flowering season for your plants will vary. In the UK, Japanese indigo flowers in the late autumn and the seeds are ready to collect in October. Sometimes the flowers haven't matured enough before the first frost, so I have successfully picked the flower stems, placed in jars of water and brought them indoors. When it comes to collecting seeds, look for shiny dark brown seeds, then snip off the whole top of the plant. You can then gently run your fingers along the flower heads to release the seeds.

Further indigo dyeing

This simple fresh leaf experiment is just the beginning; it's a taster of what this beautiful plant has to offer! For more comprehensive indigo studies (including fermented indigo vats) take a look at:

- Liz Spencer **thedogwooddyer.com**
- Britt Boles **indigofest.org**

Making watercolours from earth

Forage for ochres in your local area and transform the pigments into watercolour paint.

Words and photos by Clara Infante

If you look around when you're driving or taking a walk in nature, you'll notice there is a wide array of colours in the ground. Ochre was used for painting walls in the ancient Mediterranean world and it is one of the main pigments used in Australian indigenous art. The advantage of using earth pigments is that most are thousands of years old and light fast, meaning they won't fade in sunlight.

When foraging, I like to bring a paint brush and a drawing pad with me. You can do the same: test the earth you've found by wetting it and painting on paper, then you can decide if you'd like to collect any. I keep my foraged materials in small plastic bags which I label with the date and location. This way I can find the colours again.

Safely foraging for ochres

Clay or ground earth are the safest options to use when making watercolours, which I recommend especially for beginners. Ochres offer a wide range of colours and can be easily identified. You'll typically find ochre in shades of yellow, orange, red and purple in bands along road cuts. The earth will often feel like dry clay and is usually rich in sand or clay.

You will find earth on the side of the road, near river banks and other places where erosion occurs, but please do your research before you begin foraging as some locations may be protected, even if they're not a park or nature reserve.

Safety: Ochres are safe to handle provided you wear a protective face mask when processing the earth. Grinding unidentified stones can be toxic, so until you can accurately identify rocks, stick to earth and ochres. Stones and earth may have levels of toxicity which may be harmful to your lungs after repeated exposure. When working with earth, ochres or any other pigments, ensure you wear a mask and work in a well ventilated area.

PLANT FORAGE MAKE

Basic tools & items you'll need

- A small handful of earth
- Tap water
- A jar with a lid
- A sieve and fine mesh scrap fabric, e.g. cheesecloth
- A glass or marble slab to use as a surface to mull your paint (you can also use old floor tiles)
- A muller or alternatively a glass object with a thick flat bottom, e.g. a glass candelabra
- Painters palette knives
- Tin or plastic watercolour pans to put your paints in once you have finished. Alternatively, you can put your watercolours in seashells!
- Two or more containers, preferably with a bit of transparency so you can see into the water and earth you're working with
- A spoon to scoop out impurities
- An oven dish or pan to dry your pigment
- A pestle and mortar for grinding your pigments
- A safety mask

PLANT FORAGE MAKE

Making your binder

A binder is the substance that the pigment is mixed into in order to create paint. You can use a wide array of binders to make paints. I recommend using gum arabic (made from the sap of the acacia tree), and mixing it with honey or vegetable glycerin. You can also use egg whites or tree gum if you're aiming for something that hasn't been processed at all. As a preservative, you'll need tea tree or clove essential oil.

I make my binder the day before I mix my paints. Some people like to let their binder set for longer, 24-48 hours is pretty standard. Once you've mixed the ingredients, I suggest putting the binder in the refrigerator to keep it from going off, though the essential oils will help to preserve it for around a month.

I use 4 parts liquid gum arabic to 1 part glycerin, plus 2 - 3 drops of clove oil. If you're working with dry gum arabic, I suggest mixing 4 parts hot water with 2 parts gum arabic and 1 part glycerin.

There are other types of tree sap that can work if you're hoping to forage your own binder; I can personally recommend apricot tree gum.

You can replace glycerin with honey or use a mixture of the two if you're experimenting with making different binders to your liking. Glycerin acts as a humectant; it makes the paint more flexible and less brittle.

Processing earth pigments

Once you've collected a handful of earth, you can put it in a jar with 6 times the amount of water. Then put the lid on the jar and shake it up as much as you can over 20 minutes, turning the jar upside down and right side up to wet your earth as much as possible. Once you set down your jar, the impurities in the earth should float up to the top (e.g. small twigs, roots and insects) and you can scoop them out with a spoon.

Photo A shows the earth after it's been washed and has been sitting overnight. The bottom layer is the soil and the layer above is the pigment. Above that you can see the water is completely clear and at the very top are impurities that have floated up.

A.

Levigating

Levigating involves filtering the pigment with consecutive water baths. Once you've cleaned your earth, you should continue to shake your container. I like to leave my earth in the water over night. The next day, you'll see a heavy layer of clay at the bottom of your vessel and a thin layer of pigment at the top. You can pour the top layer of water and pigment into your second container and passing it through a cheesecloth, which will keep the earth from passing into that second container and help separate the pigment from the earth particles.

Photo B shows the liquid being poured through a cheesecloth into an empty container. The soil is heavy and should stay put inside the mason jar, but if any soil does try to make its way from one container to the other, the cheesecloth will keep it from doing so.

B.

Once you have done this with all of your earth, you can repeat the process, adding water to your earth and shaking it, allowing another pigment layer to form and separating it again. Your pigment jar should now have a thin layer of earth pigment sitting at the bottom. Without agitating it, carefully pour all of the clear water out of the container, avoiding draining any of your pigment with it.

Photo C: You've separated your pigment from the soil, you can now wait for it to drop down to the bottom of your new container and repeat the process with your left over soil as many times as you'd like.

Photo D: Now your pigment is sitting at the bottom of your container, you can carefully pour the clear water out without agitating your pigment too much. Once the pigment tries to make its way out of the container, you can pour water and pigment into an oven dish or flat pan to dry. Leave it to dry somewhere warm so the water evaporates.

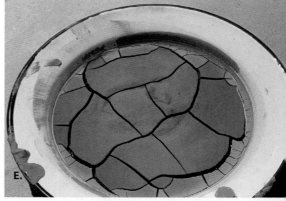

Photo E shows the dry pigment. Depending on the weather conditions and the amount of pigment, it can take a couple of hours or days to dry, it will crack and curl up on the pan. This is your levigated pigment.

Photo F shows the pigment being ground with a pestle and mortar. Safety reminder: work in a well ventilated area and wear a mask to protect your lungs from fine particles.

Once its in powder form, you can store it or use it straight away.

Mulling your watercolours

The mulling process helps break down your pigments into finer particles but is mainly designed to help the pigment and oils in the binder bond.

Remember to wear a mask to protect your lungs from fine particles and work somewhere with good circulation.

I always recommend starting small, as mulling can be a physical and tiresome task.

Start by adding 1 tablespoon of pigment onto your slab, make a hole in the centre of your mound and pour approximately ½ teaspoon of your binder into it.

Take your palette knife and mix in the binder, pouring more over the paste as you go until you've reached a creamy consistency.

Start moving your muller in circles. Your pigment needs a bit of time to soak in the binder. All pigments react differently to the amount of binder being used. Those with a higher earth content (ochres) will require more binder than ones richer in iron. Try not to add too much binder or you'll have a very liquid mixture which will take a very long time to dry and when it does, it will shrink down significantly in your pan.

Once you've mulled your mixture into a thin layer covering your work surface, you can take your palette knife and scoop it back into the centre of your slab and start again. Repeat this process until you have a smooth mixture if that is your desired result. Not all pigments will need to be mulled for the same amount of time; some require more effort than others.

Filling your pans

Once you have a homogenous mixture, you can scoop it with your palette knife and pour it into your pans or seashells. Paints also vary in drying times depending on the pigment and the weather. You can use a low temperature dehydrator to help speed the process along!

Further reading

For more information on making earth pigments, read *The Organic Artist* by Nick Neddo and visit Karen Vaughan's website *theartofsoil.com*.

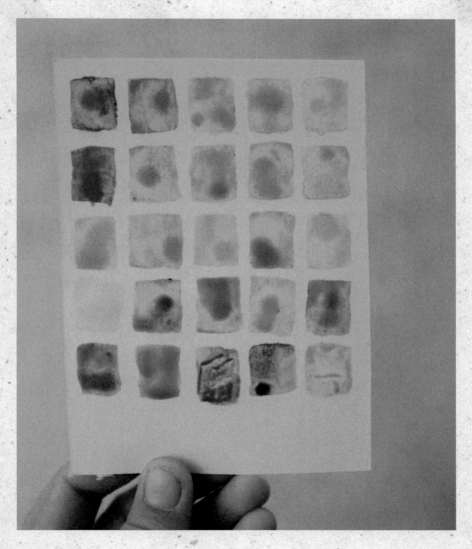

PLANT FORAGE MAKE

"(...) life over the last few years has shown me something:
that, when you begin to tune in to your surroundings and to notice the shifts throughout the year, you learn a new language, that of the natural world around you. I believe that nature can be found everywhere, even in the cracks on the pavement, and that we all have the ability to feel at home and secure in a sense of belonging to the places we inhabit. Sometimes, we just need the right tools to unlock this warm sense of kinship."

– taken from *The Wild Craft* by Catarina Seixas,
published by Hardie Grant Books.

Freshly picked

Join us for an interview with Colleen Codekas from Grow, Forage, Cook, Ferment!

Words and photos by Colleen Codekas

I often hear people say that "foraging is a superpower", which feels quite fitting as it's pretty special being able to search for sustenance in the wild. How does foraging make you feel?

In a word: empowered. It is so empowering to be able to identify, harvest, and use edible and medicinal wild plants!

Can you share a bit about your journey and how you first got into the world of plants and herbs?

I've always loved being out in nature and foraging just became an extension of that. It started with simply learning to identify the plants and trees I would see while hiking. Then I got a job in Yosemite National Park, which is where I learned about elderberry and yarrow and their benefits. I also found morel mushrooms, king boletes, and wild onions, which was very exciting! It just grew from there and eventually I started foraging a lot of different plants in Oregon when we lived there. I started my blog, *Grow Forage Cook Ferment* soon after that and have never stopped foraging and learning about plants!

What are your top three edible wild plants that you'd love to teach everyone to identify?

This is hard to answer because it depends on where I am and what season it is! In general though, I would say purple dead nettle because most people have seen it but they don't realise it is edible, chanterelle mushrooms because they are so fun to find and delicious, and rose hips because they are so common and full of health benefits.

PLANT FORAGE MAKE

Clockwise: dandelion, chickweed, wild violets, yarrow & purple dead nettle.

What are the benefits of living and eating with the seasons?

I find that it really connects you to the land and region that you are living in. There is always something new that will be popping up through the seasons, which makes it fun and special. Plus there are so many health benefits from eating freshly picked wild foods!

I imagine your cupboards are a treasure chest of beautiful coloured bottles with infusions of oil, honey, vinegar and jars of ferments. Are the colours in plants and flowers an indicator of their nutritional value or potency?

I do have many jars of wonderful plant concoctions, it's true! I believe in many cases the vibrancy of plants does indicate nutritional value or potency. Often the colours are from antioxidants, carotenoids, and flavonoids which are all highly beneficial. That said, things like roots may not be super colourful, but they can still have a lot of vitamins and minerals and other benefits. Dandelion root is one example!

What's the safest way to learn how to identify wild plants?

If local walks are available in your region that is always a good option, as is going with a friend who knows how to identify edible and medicinal plants. It's always preferable to see the plant in person if possible. I think regional book guides are also very useful – this is how I mostly learned. Websites and courses can be very helpful too, but nothing beats seeing the plants in real life.

Left to right: rosehips, purple dead nettles and elderberries.

PLANT FORAGE MAKE

What are you particularly looking forward to growing in your garden this year?

We just recently moved from Oregon to Vermont, so our whole garden will be new this year! I'm hoping to plant an extensive herb garden and am hoping to include some plants that are common to this region such as valerian and jewelweed. I'm also excited to get some lilac shrubs and berry bushes planted!

Can you share any tips for growing edible crops in a small garden?

My main tips would be to only grow what you love to eat and plant a little more densely than you think! I love the square foot gardening method for small gardens.

Do you enjoy the creative challenge of working with plants?

I really do, although I don't find it too much of a "challenge" because I love the work so much. The most challenging part is the short season of many plants - I have to get to them while they are out and ready!

Is there anything else you'd like to share with us about you or your work?

Just that being out in nature is so rewarding no matter what you are doing! I love teaching people that all they really need to do is get outside. Even if you aren't foraging, there is so much benefit to just being with the plants. It really is one of the best things you can do for your physical and mental health! 🌿

Butterfly pea flowers

Try growing these beautiful blue blooms in your garden to use as natural food colouring in tasty treats you make in the kitchen!

Words by Tara Lanich-LaBrie

Butterfly pea flower, *Clitoria ternetea,* has been used across the globe for thousands of years. I use this prolific vining plant in many of my treats and savoury meals. The colour is impressively heat-stable. Butterfly pea flowers impart a beautiful blue colour to foods and drinks, which, like other anthocyanin-rich colours, turns pink/purple with the addition of an acid, such as lemon juice.

The flowers dry very well and can be turned into a powder using a spice grinder, which is convenient to use in the kitchen. You can also buy butterfly pea flowers from some online speciality shops.

Powerful colour

Many years ago, I dreamed of growing a farm wholly dedicated to blue and purple-hued plants. Although that was not the route I took, my fascination and love grew for these anthocyanin-rich plants. Blue is one of the rarest colours in nature for edible food. Blueberries are the exception, and they are of course, excellent for our health. In a typical grocery store in the western world, a large portion of the food is white, tan or brown in colour. Blue and purple coloured foods are the least eaten foods.

Anthocyanins, the compounds that are responsible for the vibrant blue hue of these flowers, are a class of water-soluble flavonoids. Anthocyanins are bioactive compounds with incredible health benefits.

Grow your own

Butterfly pea flowers grow relatively well in a variety of climates with a little help from you! If you have space outside with direct sunlight, or you have enough room for pots, then you can grow them! They do love well-drained soil and regular watering in the beginning, but they are actually relatively drought tolerant.

This plant is native to tropical areas and it will definitely grow best there, but it can be grown all over the world. I live in Colorado at a relatively high altitude and my growing season is very short with deep frosts and snow possible in the months of May and September. I also grew this beautiful plant in New Mexico at an even higher altitude. It requires a slightly different approach, but it blooms prolifically once it gets going.

Find seeds online the first year, then save your own seeds for the future planting. Sow into well-drained pots, start seeds in seedling trays or direct sow. I like to start my seeds ahead of time in an effort to get them very strong and healthy before setting them into the ground.

When you transplant, pick a sunny place and dig a hole about twice as large as your transplant. Place your seedling in the hole, then pack the soil around the plant so a good portion of the stem sits below the soil level.

As these are vining plants, they will need a trellis, fence or stands to climb and wind around. In tropical climates, they can grow to 6-10 feet in height and will bush out about 2-3 feet at their largest. My plants are usually fairly short as we have a short growing season.

Drying flowers

Collect the flowers every couple of days and lay them on a plate or screen to dry. While your flowers are drying, flip them over every 8 hours so they dry evenly. I wait several days to a week until they are completely dry before putting them into a sealed glass jar in a dark cabinet.

Saving seeds

Let the pods grow and turn tan-brown before harvesting the peas. Store in a paper envelope, in a cool, dark place until you're ready to sow the following year.

Top photo from iStock, lower 2 photos by Tara.

PLANT FORAGE MAKE

Spiced chai latte

Words and photo by Tara Lanich-LaBrie

This bright blue, spiced drink is excellent for giving your body a gentle boost.

I love to make this milky drink on a cool and dewy spring morning, stirring the brew, wafting delicious smells throughout the house. This flavourful, caffeine-free blend starts with kitchen spices like cinnamon and peppercorns, and builds with favourite adaptogenic herbs, such as tulsi (holy basil) and butterfly pea flowers. Adaptogenic plants are simultaneously energising and stress relieving, without the buzz of caffeine.

This recipe includes calendula which is a sip of the sun, embodying the warmth of summer days in every flower ray. Rosehips are packed with vitamin C and they add a berry-like sweetness to the blend. Enjoy this colourful drink as an occasional treat.

PLANT FORAGE MAKE

Butterfly pea flower chai recipe

Adjust this recipe depending on what you have in your kitchen, so feel free to make substitutions or leave things out. This makes enough for 2 people.

Ingredients

10 oz (284 ml) water
8 oz (227 ml) milk of your choice
1 tsp vanilla extract
1 tbsp dried butterfly pea flowers (or 6 fresh flowers)
1 tbsp calendula flowers, dried
2 tbsp fresh ginger, peeled and chopped or ½ tsp dried ginger
2 tsp rosehips or 2 tbsp whole fresh rosehips
2 tsp rose petals, dried
½ tsp tulsi (holy basil)
1 cinnamon stick or ½ tsp cinnamon powder
1/8 tsp fennel seeds
1/8 tsp coriander seeds
1/2 tsp black peppercorns
2 crushed cardamom pods or ¼ tsp ground cardamom

Optional: rose petals and nettle seeds for topping, and sweetener of your choice.

Directions

- In a medium saucepan, warm the water, milk, rosehips, ginger, peppercorns, fennel, cardamom, coriander seeds and cinnamon.
- Bring to a simmer and cover, stirring occasionally for about 8 minutes.
- Uncover the saucepan, then add the tulsi, rose petals, butterfly pea flowers and calendula. Simmer lightly for 1-2 minutes with the cover on, then turn off the heat, leaving the pan on the stove top.
- Stir in the vanilla extract and cover the pan, letting it steep for at least 10-20 minutes.
- Strain through a fine mesh sieve or coffee filter. Warm the strained liquid if needed and sweeten to taste.
- Sprinkle with rose petals, nettle seeds or cinnamon powder and enjoy! 🌿

Safety guidance: This recipe isn't a way to ingest herbs on a daily basis; this is simply a drink to be enjoyed as an occasional treat. If you are pregnant, breastfeeding, have any underlying health conditions or are taking any medication, you should talk to your doctor before ingesting any herbs. Please consult a qualified herbalist for treating with herbs.

Rainbow Socca Pancakes

Treat yourself to these colourful and delicious pancakes and incorporate your local wild edibles into the batter.

Words and photos by Tara Lanich-LaBrie

Socca is a delicious and easy savoury kind of pancake that comes from France, with other versions originating in Italy under the name Farinata or Torta de Ceci. Traditionally this would be cooked over an open fire or grilled in large pans, but it works in a high heat oven and is incredibly versatile! The first socca I ever made years ago was bright green with kale and basil from my garden, and I was inspired to add different colours and plants to the batter this time to make a palette of colour and flavour that welcomes spring. These can be as simple as you have time for, or as complex as you can imagine. I quadrupled the base recipe and turned each one into a different colour.

Ingredients

1 cup besan flour (chickpea/garbanzo bean flour)
1 cup water
6 tbsp olive oil (reserve some to brush on top)
1 tsp sea salt
Cracked black pepper to taste
Optional toppings: fresh or dried herbs, flowers, mushrooms, cherry tomatoes (I used husk cherries, a yellow low-growing fruit that is slightly different to a tomato, but related)

To make the colours

- Red: ¼ cup beetroot (beet) juice substituted in for the water. So, ¼ cup beetroot juice and ¾ cup water instead of the full cup of water.

- Blue: 2 tsp blue spirulina and 1 tsp butterfly pea flower powder added to the batter.

- Green: 2 tbsp powdered nettles and 2 droppers of concentrated liquid chlorophyll.

- Yellow: 2 tsp turmeric powder and 2 tsp yellow curry powder.

Preparations

- Preheat the oven to 475°F (240°C or 10°C lower for a fan assisted oven). Place a rack almost as high as it can go in the oven and put your cast iron skillet in there. Use a small skillet if you're making several small pancakes, or you can make one large one with the recipe in a 10-12 inch skillet.
- As I mentioned before, I quadrupled the recipe to split it into four.
- To make the batter, whisk or blend the besan flour, salt, cracked black pepper, water, and 3 tbsp of the olive oil. Make sure you whisk or blend until all the clumps are totally smooth and the overall texture is like heavy cream.
- Now add the ingredients in four separate bowls for the four different colours/flavours.
- Remove the skillet from the oven and pour enough olive oil to completely coat the bottom of the pan.
- Pour in approximately 1/3 of the mixture of one of the socca batters into a smaller skillet. Alternatively, add the entire batter of one colour into a larger skillet. Quickly add any flowers, herbs or mushrooms in a design, and place the whole thing into the oven for 7-10 minutes.
- Check to see if it is getting solid, and when it is, remove quickly and brush the top with olive oil, before putting it back in the oven for just a few more minutes, until the edges begin to get crisp and golden brown.
- Remove and serve with the tomato sauce (or another sauce of your choice) or enjoy with a crisp salad!

"These can be as simple as you have time for, or as complex as you can imagine."

Savory Tomato Sauce, based on Salsa Rojo

Ingredients

3 tbsp olive oil
¼ cup onion, chopped
1 clove garlic, chopped
2 cups tomatoes peeled, seeded and chopped
2 tsp dried oregano or *Monarda fistulosa* (also known as wild oregano or wild bee balm), dried or fresh. If using fresh, add 2 tbsp.
Salt and pepper, to taste
Optional: a sprinkle of cayenne pepper

Preparations

- Preheat the oven to 400°F (200°C) and get out a baking sheet.
- Add tomatoes, onions and garlic to the baking sheet and coat in olive oil.
- Roast for 10-15 minutes, or until the tomatoes "melt" and the onions get softer.
- Scoop them into a blender, and add the oregano, salt and pepper, and a sprinkle of cayenne pepper for a little heat.
- Blend on high, and pour into a bowl to serve with the socca!

Foraged Fibres

Suzie Grieve is a wild weaver who creates intricately detailed baskets and jewellery from foraged fibres.

Words and photos by Suzie Grieve

Hi Suzie. Can you tell us a bit about how you started weaving?

It was a few years ago now, whilst feeling a bit lost in this crazy world of ours and in need of direction, that I sat and had a long think about what it was I wanted to spend my days learning about. Plants of course! They are beautiful beings and absolutely integral to our existence.

So, I dedicated myself to making my own little plant education. I started by buying myself an Identification book and meticulously going through the pages, getting to

know the plants and their families and collecting and pressing many of them.

Then came the foraging... which was around the same time that I joined my first community. This was a beautiful period of time. A time when I met many other plant and nature obsessed people who taught me many, many things and opened my mind to different ways of living. We spent our days planting potatoes, singing songs, telling stories, making massive wild salads of chickweed, dandelion, chenopod and sorrel and learning about herbal medicine together. There were always herbs hanging to dry and big pots of herbal infusions brewing on the fire.

The first weaving came about one day when I was mulling over how I was going to build the new vegetable beds. I wanted to use the materials we had on the land and nothing was more

abundant than hazel. The first veggie bed of the woven hazel was rubbish but pretty quickly my hands took to the simple repetitive motions and I fell in love. This new tactile way of connecting with plants had hooked me – the smells, the textures, the movements, the whole process fascinated me.

I spent the next few years on the road without much of a base, so it was only when I got back home to Cumbria that I could really immerse myself in this new-found passion of tangling plants and their leaves, vines, roots, bark and stems.

What are some of your favourite locally foraged fibres to work with?

Ahhh, such a difficult question! There are so many favourites... ivy, bramble, bindweed, iris, willow bark, dandelion, juncus, cattail, I could go on!

I especially get a lot of joy from turning plants that others often see as weeds into useful or beautiful little vessels. They are often overlooked or even disliked, but their strength, flexibility, resilience and abundance make them awesome weavers!

Although I don't have firm favourites, dandelions do have a special place in my heart. Gathered after they have flowered and seeded, the left over stems dry to a shiny golden colour and always make me happy when I weave with them.

Are there general guidelines for processing fibres? Can you share part of your process with us?

Gathering and preparing your own fibres for weaving can be a crazy lengthy process but in the end it's a very satisfying one. The process starts by getting to know your local area, the plants and the land they grow on. Check which plants grow in abundance, maybe you know a particularly unruly patch of brambles, a tree dangling with Ivy or a hedgerow full of bindweed. Maybe you have a garden full of leaves like crocosmia, daylily or daffodils.

Then, harvest seasonally. It's important to pay attention to the time of year. These are the general guideline that I follow:

- Winter: vines & sticks
- Spring: bark
- Summer: stems
- Autumn: leaves

Once you have gathered the material, it's necessary to dry everything fully. This allows the plants to do all the shrinking they are going to do before it comes to

weaving. If you weave with fresh leaves and vines you will end up with a wobbly basket.

Drying the plants also lets you store the material until you have time to do the weaving.

When the time does eventually come to tangle up those leaves or vines, they must be rehydrated. This can range from a quick dip in water, to being submerged for a whole day depending on the plant, size of the material and temperature of the water etc. There are a lot of nuances to the whole process but you'll find what works for you and hopefully have fun in the process.

You're known for making incredibly detailed, miniature baskets. What do you most enjoy about working on a tiny scale?

One of the simple reasons I work in miniature, creating tiny baskets and woven necklaces, is the lack of space to grow or store massive amounts of materials. Every single leaf I weave into one of my baskets has been gathered, hung and dried. It's a slow process and a

" The process starts by getting to know your local area, the plants and the land they grow on."

slow craft! Also, weaving smaller baskets means I can explore many different techniques, styles and types of basket with what I have available to me and with the space I currently have! Though, to be honest, if somehow I did find myself with a massive weaving barn I would still make tiny baskets, I would just have more space to dance around whilst doing so.

The range of colours in your baskets is captivating. Do you enjoy playing with colour and pattern in your creations?

Thank you! Yes! I love all the different subtle colours and textures of the different plant fibres. It's really made me appreciate quite how many different greens and browns there are!

I especially enjoy combining the different plants together in one basket and creating simple patterns or stripes.

It really accentuates the already mesmerising patterns of the weaving itself.

Although I love the natural palette of the plant fibres, I would love to try dyeing some willow bark sometime!

Like with natural dyes, do some of the coloured fibres change or mature over time? Have you ever had any surprises?

Many of the fibres change colour over time, especially if they sit in the sun. Some fibres will fade and some will darken. It's been interesting to see.

Dandelion and iris are beautiful after a year or two; they loose all their green and become a beautiful shiny gold, Daylily leaves fade to a warm yellow, willow bark slowly becomes orangey

PLANT FORAGE MAKE

brown and cattail leaves fade to an almost khaki/beige matt colour.

What's the most unexpected plant fibre that you've enjoyed weaving with?

Once you get into fibres it really does seem like they're lurking everywhere! You start getting curious about your house plants and even the vegetables as you're preparing dinner. Pineapple, corn, horseradish and lemongrass all have interesting and usable fibres but my favourite fibre discovery was probably rhubarb. It was whilst I was peeling a few stems of their bright pink skin I had the idea for weaving, so put a handful aside to dry. Although not the strongest fibre, it makes the most stunning pink tiny baskets and cordage!

Do you also feel passionate about foraging edible plants for food?

Of course! There's nothing better than going foraging with your own foraged basket.

Being winter at the moment there's not been so much about but there's always something! I try to follow the *'eat at least one wild thing a day'* rule. Even if it's a single rosehip or a couple of dandelion leaves. Soon, though, the wild greens will be here in abundance, starting with the wild garlic and cleavers which are already starting to poke their heads up! I think It's such a valuable skill to be able to forage sustainably, especially with how the world's currently going. I think it's crazy and a bit sad that we're not all teaching ourselves and children these basic human skills like foraging and

growing our own food that would allow us to live more sustainably.

Is there anything else you'd like to tell us about you or your work?

For the past year or so I've been working on a wild basketry book. I thought it was about time I gathered all I have learnt about the plants and their fibres and get it down on some paper!

When I started, I didn't realise quite how big it was going to be but there's so much to get in there. Each plant deserves a book of its own! The first section will be taking each plant in detail, its uses, history and folklore. Followed by instructions on the gathering, processing, drying and rehydrating of the plant and all its fibre and basketry uses.

The second section of the book will be tutorials on different wild basket projects and techniques.

It's been tricky to keep on top of the photos, as living in Cumbria days without rain are rare but we're nearly there! 🌿

Visit Suzie's website: foragedfibres.co.uk

"It's such a valuable skill to be able to forage sustainably, especially with how the world's currently going."

PLANT FORAGE MAKE

Photo by Markus Winkler

Dandelion pesto

A weed is a matter of perspective! The humble dandelion is often considered a nuisance, but with a bit of knowledge and appreciation, perhaps this resilient plant might just win you over. Give chlorophyll-rich dandelion leaves a try by making a fresh pesto.

Words by Harmonie O'Loughlin

Nutritional benefits

Did you know that all parts of dandelion are edible and have medicinal value to the herbalist? In the following recipe we will be using the vibrant green leaves which contain calcium, potassium and Vitamins A, C, B and D. The bitter leaves stimulate the digestive system – bitter flavours are uncommon in the modern diet, so tap into its bitter taste as a tonic in spring.

Foraging tips

Dandelion is pure abundance. You do not have to look far for a place to harvest, but ensure the area has not been sprayed with chemicals. Also be mindful that it isn't too close to a road. Richly hued dandelion leaves stand out amongst the spring grasses in your lawn. Look for those sharply jagged edges that form a rosette. Pick when they are vividly green and free of pest bites.

"Dandelions are just friendly little weeds who only want to be loved like flowers." – Heather Babcock

Photos by Harmonie O'Loughlin

Spring is the time to incorporate wild greens into your diet. Instinctually, we crave light, nutrient dense foods after a winter of heavy meals. Young spring leaves are a little less bitter and a great way to explore this taste.

Compared to the typical basil version, this pesto has a bit of a zing and yet a more neutral taste profile.

Try this recipe as a condiment, dip, within a creamy grilled cheese sandwich or atop sweet, caramelized vegetables as a lively contrast.

PLANT FORAGE MAKE

Dandelion pesto

1/4 cup pine nuts
1/2 cup parmesan, shredded
1 garlic clove
3 cups dandelion leaves
1 tsp salt
1/3 cup or more of extra virgin olive oil
Optional: dandelion flowers

- Toast pine nuts at 350°F (170°C) for 5 minutes.
- Using a food processor, blend pine nuts into a paste.
- Whirl in parmesan and garlic.
- Whirl in dandelion leaves and salt.
- Slowly pour in olive oil until you reach your desired texture.
- Pour into a bowl and adorn with dandelion flower petals for a secondary burst of colour.

Vegan recipe

3/4 cup cashews
1/4 cup pine nuts
1/4 cup nutritional yeast
1 garlic clove
3 cups dandelion leaves
1 tsp salt
1/3 cup or more of extra virgin olive oil
Optional: dandelion flowers

- Cover cashews with water and soak for 4 hours or overnight. Strain.
- Toast pine nuts at 350°F (170°C) for 5 minutes.
- Using a food processor, blend the cashews and pine nuts into a paste.
- Whirl in nutritional yeast and garlic.
- Whirl in dandelion leaves and salt.
- Slowly pour in olive oil until you reach your desired texture.
- Pour into a bowl and sprinkle with dandelion flower petals for a pop of colour.

Violet syrup

After a long winter, it's pure delight to spend an afternoon foraging violets with the light spring breeze and sweet smell of fresh grass.

Making violet syrup gives you such versatility in the kitchen. The naturally sweet flavour will dazzle in drinks and desserts. It's delicious in homemade lemonade or gin and tonic, and is a yummy ice cream topper alone or stewed with fresh blueberries.

Words and photos by Harmonie O'Loughlin

What makes violets purple? It's the components of pigment within the plant! Purple coloured plants contain a higher concentration of anthocyanin compared to higher levels of chlorophyll in green ones. Have white violets in your yard? Like hydrangeas, violets may be sensitive to the acidity of the soil. The less acidic it is, the more likely the flowers will be white. However, even white violets, due to their purple veins, will bestow a light blue tint to the tea used to make this syrup. It is still worth making for flavour alone!

Watch as the colour immediately imparts itself in the tea. Adding sugar subdues the shade, but that is only short-lived. With a few drops of lemon juice squeezed into the syrup, the violet's true vibrancy shines once more. The anthocyanin pigment is pH sensitive and the colour turns pink with acid! Play with this feature and create colour-changing drinks and desserts with a squeeze of lemon juice!

PLANT FORAGE MAKE

Ingredients

1 cup violet petals
1 cup water
1 cup sugar
1 lemon
8 oz canning jar

Preparations

- Fill jar with petals and top with boiling water.
- Cover and steep for 24 hours.
- Strain petals.
- In a pan, heat equal amounts of the violet tea infusion and sugar, until the sugar has dissolved.
- Pour into a bottle and let the syrup cool.
- Cut a lemon in half and squeeze into syrup.
- Watch in amazement as the colour shifts to a beautiful pink hue.

Notes

- Use more or less violets depending on how they fit within the jar.
- Use half a lemon per cup of syrup.
- Store in fridge for up to a month or freeze for extended shelf life.
- An alternative sweetener may be used, but cane sugar is best when working with flowers as the neutral flavour allows you most readily to taste the blooms.

PLANT FORAGE MAKE

Photo by Katie Moum

PLANT FORAGE MAKE

"As long as autumn lasts,
I shall not have hands,
canvas, and colours enough
to paint the beautiful
things I see."

– Vincent Van Gogh

A daily colour practice

Pick up a paint brush for few minutes each day and record the colours you see in nature.

Words and photos by Lorene Edwards Forkner

Colour is about seduction. It is both a delightful gift and one of nature's most sophisticated tools designed to capture the attention of all living creatures. I like to say that colour is my love language, a universal tongue that allows me to connect with anyone across all borders and barriers. Along with pollinators searching for pollen and nectar and hungry animals foraging for ripe fruit, we humans are living creatures under the spell of colour.

I am an artist as well as a writer who gardens and a gardener who writes. Making a garden is like being inside a work of art as it's being created. I paint pictures with plants, sculpt the landscape and choreograph moments in time.

I began recording the colours in my garden with watercolour shortly after the death of my father in early 2018. What began as a simple exercise to distract from heartbreak, has since become essential, a meditative daily practice that quiets my mind.

Anything that encourages us to slow down and pay attention is nourishing.

My daily colour practice is very simple, and I encourage you to pick up a brush and join me. You don't need fancy paint. I began by using what I had on hand, a craft store watercolour set with chalky pigments that were more garish than garden. But with use, I became familiar with mixing my paints to express what I was seeing. Later, I treated myself to finer paints with more saturated pigments and nuanced colours. Would I go back? Probably not, but I learned a great deal exploring the range and limitation of that original, humble palette.

There's a delightful feedback loop to identifying colour. The more we look, the more we see. Flexing our perception helps us to reframe the familiar. So, when you sit down to create a colour study, try to forget, just for a moment, what you think you know and concentrate on seeing what is right in front of you. A plum blossom, a mussel shell, even a scrap of moss, all contain almost infinite subtleties and nuance.

heavenly hydrangea

"Anything that encourages
us to slow down and pay
attention is nourishing."

Let's begin painting

Place your chosen subject on a piece of white paper. This helps eliminate distraction and reveal details. I create my colour studies on 140# cold press watercolour paper that has a pebbled, organic feel. Of course, you'll need a brush. I use a water brush with a square head that makes it easy for me to create my familiar grid of swatches. Experiment to find your own mark.

A good place to begin mixing and matching colour is to determine whether the hue is warm or cool. Obviously, I don't mean a literal temperature, just its overall cast. Warm colours shift toward yellow—think warmth of the sun. Cool colours lean blue—think chill of the night. When in doubt as to whether a colour is warm or cool, it helps to compare it to another version of itself. Look closely at this colour study of a florist cyclamen (below). The plant's petals contain both warm and cool versions of pink.

Naming both expands and specifies our perception of colour. And it's fun! What's more, naming colours puts us into a conversation with others. If you say orange, we both probably picture an orange, orange. But if you say peach, apricot, tangerine, or pumpkin, suddenly, you've helped me to "see" various expressions of what is still, basically orange.

When you're satisfied with your mixing, lay down a swatch to record your colour. I love the immediacy and luminosity of watercolour, the way you can build up sheer washy layers to develop depth and nuance. That said, it can be an unforgiving medium. Keep a light touch. Don't fuss over a colour that's not working. Trust me, you'll only end up with a muddy mix and your watercolour paper will begin to shred. Colour can't be forced.

Over the years that I've been creating these colour studies, I've come to the

84 cyclamen

PLANT FORAGE MAKE

rather obvious conclusion that nature does this much better than I ever will. Be kind to yourself as you dip your brush and wet your paints. And remember, there's always tomorrow.

Constantly foraging for colour has taught me to be mindful of and accept my own cycles of attention. Some days flow with an almost audible chime. Others produce nothing but noise and a tiresome repetition that just about does me in.

But most days, the doing of it is enough. And there's always tomorrow—and the day after, and the one after that. The beauty of a daily practice is its constancy and its forgiveness. Over time, your colour mixing and brushwork will improve, as will your observational skills.

Learn to befriend your attention. Look with heart and compassion. Then share what you see with others. Our world needs your perspective. 🌿

*For more inspiration and encouragement, take a look at Lorene's book **Color in and Out of the Garden** (Abrams Books).*

> " *Be kind to yourself as you dip your brush and wet your paints. And remember, there's always tomorrow.* "

French breakfast

Heather

85

Photo by Autumn Mott Rodeheaver

PLANT FORAGE MAKE

The Colours of Grief

Wandering through the seasons in a year of loss.

Words by Alice Griffin

The dark humus of mud and mulch squelches beneath my feet as I walk along the towpath on a mid-winter's day. Looking down—tears pricking my eyes—it feels like the colour of grief.

Back in mid-summer grief felt blue, like the soft powdery skies. Sad but gentle, and light enough to keep breathing beneath its weight. But then, with another death—more unexpected this time—summer gave way to an autumn of deeper, more brutal hues. I found myself clinging with desperation to wisps of shimmering gold amidst dank brown, just to keep my head above ground.

Winter descended with timely hunger. I wanted (needed) to retreat from the world. Dark was only occasionally pierced by the glinting of fruit leathers—keepers of sun-ripened bounty—and the wild dancing of burnt orange in my woodburner, superimposed onto a background of a blood red sunrise over water.

I kept my focus.

And then, that day; that humus day, I finally raised my tear-filled eyes and was shocked to be lifted by the sight of a murky canal reflected with a vague stonewash blue and the brightest yellow—a singular leaf—stopping me in my tracks. The swell of my heart was instantaneous and, as if in unison, the sun poked through the heavy duvet-piled grey sky to light up the reeds. Moorhens bathed in the shallows and suddenly everything was seen beneath a lemon veil.

When submersed in the ocean that is grief, these moments of brightness in nature have saved me from drowning. They are the glints of hope guiding me forward.

Now, it is the green of new birth that sees me awaken from my winter slumber. Tree branches swathed in paper-thin lichen curl upwards, bright gold beneath the early spring sun, buds pushing out from each gnarled join. My Southernwood begins to bush and twirl and as life unfurls so do I, stretching my newness beneath bright white blackthorn blossom.

On the bow of my boat I push seeds into dirt and wait patiently for first shoots. Soon, I know, a riot of colour will erupt to lift my soul. And, just as flowers attract insects, so glimmers of life will return to my body, in time to mark the first year without two people I most preciously loved.

"On the bow of my boat I push seeds into dirt and wait patiently for first shoots. Soon, I know, a riot of colour will erupt to lift my soul."

Fruit Leather Recipe

From my friend, Therese Muskus,
Laikenbuie, Highlands of Scotland.

- Wash, drain and simmer berries (e.g. raspberries, strawberries, blackberries) in a saucepan with no extra water until soft enough to pass through a sieve. This will remove seeds for a smooth leather.
- Add 1.5 cups of puréed fruit to a blender with two mashed bananas and test for sweetness. You can add 1 tbsp of maple syrup or similar if too sharp. Aim for a thick, not runny purée.
- Spread the mixture onto a lightly oiled solid sheet and put in a dehydrator to dry for about 12 hours or until they are slightly tacky in the middle and you can peel the fruit from the oiled sheet from the edge.
- While warm cut into strips around 4 x 15 cm and roll tightly. They should stick to themselves at the end.
- Place in a clean jar and try not to eat too many at a time as it is very concentrated fruit! 🌿

Photo by Valeria Terekhina

Everlasting flowers

Grow, harvest and dry your own flowers for year-round colourful displays in your home.

Words and photos by Bex Partridge

Dried flowers or *everlastings* have gone through a resurgence over the last few years, which we could say has come at a time when there is a heightened concern for the state of the world. As we question the origins of many everyday items, dried flowers offer an alternative to 'flown flowers' as well as being a perfect filler for the winter months here in England when few flowers bloom.

For many years now, I've been growing and working with dried flowers and I'm continually experimenting to see which stems dry best and which provide the best value when growing from seed. The truth is that most flowers and foliages will dry, however some will preserve better than others. And by *better* I mean retaining their shape, colour and structure. I remain fascinated and besotted with dried flowers in equal measures. I'm in awe of the entire process of a tiny seed growing into its mother plant and then going on to dry perfectly, allowing me to weave them together into my floral designs.

The method that we use to dry flowers will affect their final appearance dramatically. It pays to take the time at the drying stage to get the best results from your stems. Next I will share some basic (but essential) rules for drying flowers. The flowers I've selected are some of the simplest to grow as well as the easiest to dry, and are the ones that I first worked with when I began this journey with everlastings.

It's all in the preparation

If you are drying flowers that you have grown yourself, the preparation of the stems is important to make sure their colour and structure are maintained. This involves cutting the best of your stems on a dry day, ideally first thing in the morning or last thing at night (avoiding the heat of the day), taking the time to strip off nearly all the unwanted leaves as you go. I tend to walk around my growing patch with a ball of string and bundle up my stems of flowers as I go, making small collections of 5-10 stems to be hung up later.

Once your stems are cut, leave them in a bucket with the end of the stems just sitting in the water to have a good drink for a few hours, or over night if cut in the evening. This ensures that your stems are in the best condition and quality before you go on to dry them.

To hang or to stand?

For the majority of botanicals the best way to dry them is by hanging them to air dry. The ideal method is to hang up high from the ceiling and away from a wall to allow air to circulate all around them. Keep the bunches away from each other to give them all space to dry out evenly. Most plants will dry fully in two to three weeks. There are a few plants that prefer to dry whilst standing upright with the stems sitting in an inch of water; these include hydrangea, gypsophila and astrantia.

As to where to dry your flowers, it can be done in any room of the house, your greenhouse or shed, so long as the following rules are followed:

Not too hot, not too cold

The temperature of the space in which you dry your flowers should be ambient, erring on the side of warmth. If the space is too cold the stems will take a very long time to dry and be susceptible to mould setting in. If the space is too warm you will find that the stems dry quickly but become brittle making them very hard to work with.

Keep out of sunlight

Whilst flowers can be dried in a light room, it is important to keep them away from direct sunlight for too long. Direct sunlight can bleach the flowers, changing their colour and appearance as well as making the stems brittle. Ideally dry away from a south facing window and up high to avoid any direct sun.

Dry all the way

The biggest issue you will find when drying flowers is mould. So wherever you choose to dry your flowers, ensure it is completely free of any moisture or dampness.

When it comes to choosing the spot to display your final display of everlastings, the same principles must be considered. This will ensure that the flowers' structure and colour remain as vibrant as when they were growing in the garden.

My top 5 flowers for colourful displays

Strawflower *(Xerochrysum bracteatum)* - salmon rose, silvery rose, purple red. These delightful sunshine flowers are the true everlastings, papery to touch as they grow, they will retain their colour and structure perfectly when dried. A must-have for all beginners.

Statice *(Limonium sinuatum)* - pastel mixed, rose light, pacific mixed, apricot beauty. Statice is another flower that falls in the true everlastings grouping. Statice now comes in a range of colours from bright blues to the softest of pinks. The colour retention is perfect.

Globe amaranth *(Gomphrena globosa)* - rose, white, pastel mix. Slightly trickier to grow from seed and get going; they tend to like dry conditions and poor soil in my experience. Beautiful delicate flower heads that are ideal for flower crowns and wreaths.

PLANT FORAGE MAKE

Xeranthemum annum *(X. annuum).* My absolute favourite flower to dry. These can be sown directly into the ground once the last frost has passed. The flower heads range from deep purple to pure white and can be cut and dried when at their peak, or allowed to go over when their petals will develop a beautiful patina of gold.

Amaranth *(Amaranthus)* - hot biscuits, coral fountain, var viridian. A showy plant that produces many stems over the course of the summer and autumn. There are a variety of different types including love-lies-bleeding which are very floppy and showy, and then there's foxtail which tends to be more upright in stature. 🌿

To learn more...

Bex's second book, *Flowers Forever* (released in June 2022) dives into her world and creative practice. With projects spanning everlasting flower meadows through to flower clouds, Bex shows you how to design stunning floral art with dried botanicals.

Paper Cosmos Flowers

Make yourself a vase of beautiful cosmos flowers. They are just as stunning as the real thing and last forever!

Words and photos by Susan Beech

Tools & materials you'll need

- General scissors & small precision scissors
- Ruler
- Card and pencil for making the template
- 160g florist crepe paper in the following colours:
  – light yellow, dark yellow and brown for the centre
  – pink or white for petals
- Doublette crepe paper in olive/light olive for leaves
- 18-gauge floral wire
- Aleene's Tacky Glue (or similar)
- Green floral tape
- Wire cutters

To make the centre

1. Cut a rectangle of crepe paper in both yellows and brown paper measuring 9 cm in length and 1.5 cm in height. Take each piece separately in your hands and with a hand on each end, pull apart to stretch the paper out completely and remove the stretch. Finely fringe one of the long edges with the scissors 3 mm deep on each of the three pieces. You can fold the piece over a couple of times to do this more quickly.

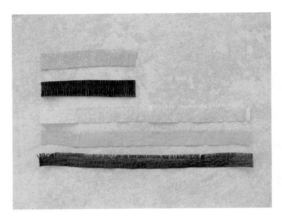

2. Apply a light line of glue across the length of one of the yellow pieces, about halfway between the base of the fine fringe and the bottom of the strip. Place the second yellow fringed piece directly on top, with the fringe on both pieces level. Then take the brown fringed piece and glue this down on top, so the fringe on this sits 1-2mm below the top of the yellow fringe.

3. Apply a little glue on the bottom left-hand side of the strip. Take a piece of 18-gauge wire and place the top point at the base of the fringe. Secure the wire at the end and then wrap the strip around the top of the wire tightly. I get a tightness on this by taking this in both my hands, pulling the strip quite tight with my right hand and with my left rolling the paper around the wire. Glue at the end to secure.

PLANT FORAGE MAKE

To make the petals

4. Next stretch a rectangle of crepe paper measuring 15 x 5 cm in your selected petal colour. Stretch this out until it won't stretch any further. Cut 8 petals per flower using the petal template. Ensure the grain of the paper runs down the length of the petal when you cut it out.

petal template: the petal measures 3.6 cm at the longest point.

5. To put the pleats in each petal, lay the petal on a flat surface and apply a thin line of glue close to the bottom edge. Then push your thumbs up against the nearest edge and gather the paper millimetre by millimetre with your other fingernails to form pleats in the paper. Use your fingernails again to scrape along the length of the petal, creasing in the lines into the paper. Bring the base of the petal to a point and twist a little to secure.

6. Next, open out the petal again, smoothing out the top third of the paper but keeping the pleats in the lower part. Place a little more glue to the twisted base and glue around the centre evenly and at the same height, just below the base of the fringing.

To make the stems & leaves

7. To cover the base of the petals, take a piece of floral tape and stretch this out to release the stickiness. Wrap around the base of the petals and then on a slight angle to cover all of the excess paper underneath the flower.

8. Then on a 45° angle, continue down the stem covering the wire. The trick with this is to try and use as little of the tape as possible and to always be on a 45° angle so the paper doesn't bulk up the stem.

9. To make leaves, cut a tall rectangle of green doublette paper, measuring 3cm wide and 6cm in height, with the grain of the paper running in the same direction as the length. Cut fine tapered slithers of paper at different heights.

10. Add a little glue to the larger base of each piece and glue these to the stem at the same height about halfway down the stem. Add another small piece of floral tape around the base of them all to secure.

11. You now have your paper cosmos and you can style it by bending the wire to bring the flowerhead forward, giving it a slight curve to the stem if you like. 🌿

PLANT FORAGE MAKE

For more paper flower projects, you'll love Susan's new book, *A Petal Unfolds*, published by Pavilion.

Photo by Gautham Krishna

Pigments in the wild

Let's explore the world of pigments
in leaves and flowers.

Words by Becky Searle

In the natural world, colour can be anything from the purely practical and utilitarian green to the flamboyant and flirtatious red. Colour can be used to attract pollinators, deter pests, or protect the plant from intense UV rays. It may seem pretty haphazard, with most well-tended gardens displaying a dazzling array of colours by summer, and sometimes even more in autumn. But colours that occur naturally on plants – in other words they haven't been selectively bred by us – are the result of thousands of years of evolution, perfecting the exact shade needed to do the job.

Let's start with green. We associate green mostly with leaves, and that is because this is where the majority of photosynthesis takes place and the pigment that makes leaves green is also the most efficient pigment for photosynthesis. The reason that the leaves appear green is because they are reflecting green light. The other types of light, like red light and blue light are absorbed and used as energy to power photosynthesis. There are lots of shades of green and it is likely that each one is specifically adapted to capture the most light in the conditions where it grows. For example, a leaf that grows in the understory of a forest may reflect a darker shade of green than a leaf growing in a meadow.

Plants will synthesise particular colours in line with the preferences of the pollinators that they want to attract. Deep, tubular flowers tend to be darker and more striking in colour to attract butterflies with long tongues, blue flowers tend to be smaller and more open to attract bees.

Butterflies can see ultraviolet, which we humans cannot see. Ultraviolet is a very short wave-length light, with a lot of energy. It is thought that butterflies can learn which flowers, and specifically which colour flowers are likely to yield the most nectar. Their ability to see shorter wave-length lights means that they are usually attracted to bright colours such as white, yellow, orange, red and purple.

Bees, on the other hand, see light completely differently and darker colours such as red will appear black to them. For that reason, they prefer longer wave-length colours such as blue and yellow.

White flowers often attract bees and butterflies, but they can also attract moths as they are easily seen in the dark. So, for each flower colour, there is an audience in mind.

Colours are of course not just to attract pollinators. Some of the most spectacular colours in nature come from leaves changing colour in autumn. It is something that a lot of us take for granted, but when we are thinking of colours in terms of their evolutionary advantage, and knowing that chlorophyll is really good at absorbing light for photosynthesis, why would the colours change when light levels start to decrease?

The answer is a little more complex than you might guess. During winter, leaves can't do much because of low light levels, so it is sometimes better for a tree to discard them than to try and hang onto them. But chlorophyll molecules are high in nitrogen, and the trees need all the nitrogen they can get to be able to create leaves and buds in the spring. So, they reabsorb the nitrogen

from chlorophyll, breaking down those green molecules. In some cases, this exposes another colour that is present in the leaves all year round, but to a lesser extent; yellow. Yellow is made from pigments called the carotenoids (think carrots!). It is not as good at absorbing light as green, but these molecules act as a sort of overflow when the chlorophyll molecules are maxed out. So, when the green is reabsorbed, the yellow becomes visible.

Other trees turn a spectacular red colour, and the way this happens is slightly different; the red comes from a group of pigments called the anthocyanins. Just like chlorophyll reflects green light, anthocyanins reflect red light. These are really high intensity, short wavelength lights that can release free radicals, those nasty things that cause us to age. So before a leaf is due to start senescing (getting ready to fall off), the tree will produce anthocyanins to protect the leaves and the chlorophyll molecules from these harmful red lights, so that the tree can absorb more nitrogen.

It may seem a little clinical to explain wonderful natural phenomenon like the vibrant colours of flowers and the gradual pallet shift in autumn in purely scientific terms. In truth, these things should be viewed with wonder and excitement. But I hope that appreciating a little of what plants do and why, can help us to experience even more wonder when we see these things. It can open our eyes to the broad spectrum of tiny miracles happening around us both in our gardens, and in the natural world. 🌿

Thanks for joining us!

Let's keep in touch...

Join my mailing list for musings on plants, creativity & simplicity:
rebeccadesnos.com/newsletter

Follow me on Instagram: **@rebeccadesnos**

Send an email: **info@rebeccadesnos.com**

Portrait by Siobhan Calder / Background photo by Robin Spielmann

Other titles published by Rebecca Desnos, also
available as eBooks via rebeccadesnos.com